MASSACRE STREET

PAUL ZITS

THE UNIVERSITY OF ALBERTA PRESS

Published by

The University of Alberta Press
Ring House 2
Edmonton, Alberta, Canada T6G 2E1
www.uap.ualberta.ca

Copyright © 2013 Paul Zits

LIBRARY AND ARCHIVES CANADA
CATALOGUING IN PUBLICATION

Zits, Paul William
      Massacre Street / Paul Zits.

(Robert Kroetsch series of Canadian
creative works)
Includes bibliographical references.
Issued also in electronic formats.
ISBN 978–0–88864–675–0

      1. Frog Lake Massacre, Frog Lake, Alta.,
1885—Poetry. 2. Frog Lake Massacre, Frog
Lake, Alta., 1885—Historiography—Poetry.
3. Cree Indians—History—Poetry. 4. Montage.
I. Title. II. Series: Robert Kroetsch series

PS8649.I87M38 2013   C811'.6
C2013–901006–8

First edition, first printing, 2013.
Printed and bound in Canada by Houghton
Boston Printers, Saskatoon, Saskatchewan.
Copyediting and proofreading by
Peter Midgley.

A volume in the Robert Kroetsch series.

The University of Alberta Press is committed
to protecting our natural environment.
As part of our efforts, this book is printed
on Enviro Paper: it contains 100% post-
consumer recycled fibres and is acid- and
chlorine-free.

The University of Alberta Press gratefully
acknowledges the support received for its
publishing program from The Canada Council
for the Arts. The University of Alberta Press
also gratefully acknowledges the financial
support of the Government of Canada
through the Canada Book Fund (CBF) and
the Government of Alberta through the
Alberta Multimedia Development Fund
(AMDF) for its publishing activities.

The settlement, by the time of its destruction in 1885, covered a large area within and bordering the Unipouheos Indian Reserve 121. The main site area of FkOo 10 is approximately 600 m east–west by 350 m north–south and is oriented along both sides of the gravel road which bisects the site. This road is probably closely aligned to the original trail to Fort Pitt and is also referred to as **'Massacre Street'** on early survey plans.

—SHEILA J. MINNI

To the gravest divine (C.B.)
and the most excitement-loving young lady (K.O.)

Method of this project: literary montage. I needn't *say* anything. Merely show it. I shall purloin no valuables, appropriate no ingenious formulations. But the rags, the refuse—these I will not inventory but allow, in the only way possible, to come into their own: by making use of them.

—WALTER BENJAMIN, from *The Arcades Project*

Often in the morning he would lie in bed and watch grids of typewritten words in front of his eyes that moved and shifted as he tried to read the words, but he never could. He thought if he could just copy these words down, which were not his own words, he might be able to put together another book and then ... yes, and then what?

—WILLIAM S. BURROUGHS, from *The Western Lands*

[H]ow unbearable it is to cut up, analyse, combine, rearrange all these texts that have now returned from silence, without ever the transfigured face of the author appearing: What! All those words, piled up one after another, all those marks made on all that paper and presented to innumerable pairs of eyes, all that concern to make them survive beyond the gesture that articulated them, so much piety expended in preserving them and inscribing them in men's memories—all that and nothing remaining of the poor hand that traced them, of the anxiety that sought appeasement in them, of that completed life that has nothing but them to survive in?

—MICHEL FOUCAULT, from *The Archaeology of Knowledge*

Contents

List of Illustrations

This Blank to be used for Commercial Messages only.

Canadian Pacific Railway Company's Tele

Sent by _____ Rec'd by

Check _____

No. _____ Time _____

By Telegraph from _____

To _____

tomb totter deea
worded learned ad
ford forbode oppos
forenoon alluding
Albert totter abah
Manœuvered withdr
tyto overbear
alterly shrunk bre
serious baking

To secure prompt despatch send reply to

I

PROLOGUE

Interview between Mr. Salamon (Sam) Pritchard and inspector
B.D. Sawyer, officer commanding North Battleford subdivision—
at Cando, Saskatchewan on March 1, 1967.

Following a rambling discussion on a variety of subjects, we came
eventually to the matter of the Frog Lake massacre. The tape takes
up the conversation at a point where we were establishing Mr.
Pritchard's age at the time of the massacre:

Tape A

i was twenty three,[1] i answered my age like
one hundred and fifth,[2] one hundred and five
now,[3] no, no,[4] i remember frog lake

the happenings, you know, around when i was
there,[5] at the time? well, i stayed mostly
always with the missionaries, they were

travelling, you know, away farther and farther
north, the missionaries with dogs, i took
the oaths, and an old priest, we go around

seeing indians, mostly all the indians,[6] yes, no
not at cold lake, but them lakes, i spend
my life quite a bit over there before i started

[1] Twenty-three, yes.
[2] You are one hundred and five now?
[3] And you would be twenty-three at Frog Lake?
[4] But you remember Frog Lake?
[5] What were you doing there at the time?
     How did you, how did you
     come to be at Frog Lake? Yes?
[6] Yes, at Cold Lake you mean, and at —?

this area,[7] hmm?[8] oh, i was at the area north
of edmonton, you know, and i,[9] yes, athabasca
and, that's where we travelled,[10] in

that country, uh huh,[11] yes,[12] yes, on they
used to call them carry all, you know, and they
were made with hides, and, oh, about that long

3

i guess, behind, where you put your stuff in[13]
and then tied from there, you know, you make
this where, for keeping your stuff in, and

the one that rides in, he rides in that carry all
and i stay behind, you know,[14] yes i stay behind[15]
i stay behind there, and with a big long rope

[7]   I see, which area was this, Mr Pritchard?
[8]   Which area was this
      that you were with the missionaries?
[9]   Ah, yes, St Albert? And Edmonton
      and Slave Lake and Athabasca? Yes?
[10] I see, I see, and you were travelling
      you were a guide for them, were you?
[11] And you drove the dogs for them, too?
[12] Did they drive the dogs themselves?
[13] Ah yes, I see, I see.
[14] He rides and you stay behind?
[15] That's no good (laughter).

sometimes i caught that, and the dogs would be
running and jump on there, and all day long
like that,[16] dogs?[17] we have six dogs,[18] yes

great big dogs, yes,[19] he was, when we, when i
lived there, the area over there, kind of long
you know, i had to drive my father to frog lake

and so i lived there,[20] about three years,[21] yeah
my dad he was working hard, uh, for them
hudson's bay too, interpreter, he was

the interpreter of the frog lake settlement
at that time, ah, so i stayed there, but i stayed
there at the church, the church was pretty close

4

[16] How many dogs in the team?
[17] Yes, how many dogs in one team?
[18] Six dogs? Oh, yes, I see.
       And your father was in Frog Lake?[a]
[19] And had you gone back to visit him
       or were you living at Frog Lake?
[20] I see, for how long?
[21] About three years, eh? I see.
       And were you helping them?
       Were you working for them?

a) John Pritchard (Interpreter, Frog Lake) would increase his already oversized load
by taking some weary one up. Pritchard and all the Breeds walked always, though by
making us walk they could have ridden. His two little boys, aged thirteen and fifteen,
walked, though their feet became very sore at times, but they never complained,
because they knew their walking enabled us to ride. They were noble little fellows.

from home, you know, i used to, used to stay
more over there than at home,[22] yes,[23] yes
fafard,[24] marchand, i think? marchand?[25] yes

i was helping them, i stayed with them mostly i
stayed more there than my dad's because
it was just a little ways from the settlement

all those that ... that lived in that frog lake
they were all government employees
some worked at the parish, and some of them

looked after the parish, and so on,[26] yes,[27] yes
quinn he was the indian agent, and delaney
was the farmer instructor, i think,[28] yes

[22] At the church?
[23] This was with Father Fafard?[b]
[24] And there was another one there, too?
[25] Yes, Father Marchand, they were there
      at the Frog Lake mission.[c]
[26] Yes, Delaney was one there.
      He was the instructor,
      the farm instructor, wasn't he?
[27] And Quinn was the agent? Big Quinn.[d]
[28] Yes, that's right, that is what Cameron
      says in his book, yes.[e]

b) Rev. Father Fafard (Catholic priest, Frog Lake) tried to push his way through the crowd
of Indians to reach the body, but they resisted. He was a wiry man and fought hard.
Travelling Spirit, however, rushed up and shot him in the chest and head, and he fell dead.
c) Rev. Father Marchand (Catholic priest, Onion Lake) was attached to Bishop Grandin's
mission, and at the time of his martyrdom was labouring in connection with Father Fafard.
d) Thomas Trueman Quinn's (Indian Agent, Frog Lake) employer's store was raided and
its owner murdered, but in the midst of these scenes of horror an Indian who had taken
a liking to young Tom Quinn's bright and handsome face hid him under the counter
among some empty salt sacks.
e) John Delaney (Farm Instructor, Frog Lake) said he had one or two [oxen].

In your reply
refer to No. ....

withold

I hold it sub [?]

Government House,

Minister of justice

Regina, ...

Sir,

      I have the honor to acknowledge the receipt of

withold it

1101
325
1426

23826
325
24151

m

abijail

      I have the honor to be,

        Sir,

        Your obedient se

Lieutenant-Governor No

To

II

THE MOUND-BUILDERS

I glanced over my shoulder from where I stood
with notebook and pencil before the scaffold and saw all this

—WILLIAM BLEASDELL CAMERON,[i]
from *The War Trail of Big Bear*[ii]

The work is a plain one

Prove fickle copious notes
Make the work comparatively easy
Endeavour to tell it plainly

A wild lonely smoke of tepee eloquence
Men naked and brown as
The narrative bald and simple

Invite the devourer
Even though the tale is not for him
To the story I have to tell

There is nothing pretty about the page
(that is all it is) yet as history
It is worth preserving

In the Long Knives' country

I had a dream, an ugly dream
I saw a spring
shooting up out of the ground
I covered it with my hand
trying to smother it, but it spurted
up between my fingers and ran
over the back of my hand

A Maundy Thursday

The zeal of your house has eaten me up
The dogs have dug me out of the land, slept their sleep, blushed for shame
They seek the root of precious things which they will trade for food
Like the wood baked into their bread, their filthiness is on them
Melts into their open mouths, their voices as arrows pass through the
    spokes of a wheel
Thunders off the tongue like a potsherd, a tongue that cleaves to a horn
In the midst of my bowels many calves reach to surround the bones that
    I have numbered
My mind, the eternal years swept of trees
Fat bulls stand on their pillars, their tongues the gates, their jaws bind
    all the festival days
We are poured out like the melted wax of kings and fetters
There is now no prophet; they have set up their ensigns for signs
They part our garments among them, and upon our vestures they cast lots
They lift up the horn

Blood galloping in his ears
welled out and flowed
down the legging
spilled on the banks of his veins
in the spring
will flow
over the back of my hand
it was a spring in his veins
his father as a young man
had paddled
of the old chief's dream
had broken forth and spurted
through his futile fingers
it's a sure sign of victory
for the Indians, always
it was an omen of bad luck

The red man whose home
this wilderness was arose
with his fierce blood galloping
in his ears
peoples
then for a time they had marvelled
and endured
and spoken in secret
the ordinary red man
the buffalo, the red man's one friend
a little later he passed our place
carrying under his arm
a box sealed with red wax
it contained the annuity money
seven thousand dollars

Hasty,
the sun would not go out
it was still high
flashing on their polished carbines
their scarlet coats aglow
against a trigger
and a flood would descend
that would drench that sunlit slope
in waves
I awoke with a start
a hand clutching my shoulder
was shaking me roughly
it was just sunrise
I sat up
permitted to see another sunset
the laugh was harsh and forced:
"a cap
I have none and the sun
is strong"

Sun-red the blood or,
The sun pushed a huge crimson shoulder above the skyline

On the morning of that day of blood
flushing it darkly as he sat looking up
from beneath his war bonnet at the old man
suddenly his right hand shot out
throwing the lever of his Winchester down
in the action of loading
and thereby raising the muzzle
and soon bad blood began
to show itself between them
howling with rage and pain
streaming down his face
and staggered blood demands blood-drunken

Eyes
dull red pools glowing murkily
in their sultry sockets
a finger, red or white
against a trigger and a flood
bedlam broke loose
the Indians went wild:
"shoot them shoot the red coat dogs"
they howled
the hotheads
"no no be careful wait let the red coats shoot first"
made much of the stately red man and the Company
for more than two hundred years
I like to see the sun get up that way
red

Red the sun blood or,
She has but half a smoke to live

Blood trickled down his leg
but he rode on
another shot
his horse stopped, swayed
a bullet in his neck
in me boils when I remember
blood gushing from her mouth
a boy named Bright Eyes stepped out
and shot the senseless skull
crying his dolorous wailing chant
because there is bad blood between the bands
and he is trying to exorcise the devils
but it starts again, very slowly
the halted blood resumes its flow
and I fall back and close my eyes once more
a horse has stumbled against the taut guy-ropes
of the lodge, that is all
and they snap like whips
that the white soldiers should come
to kill them all with their big guns
blood will tell

Man's vengeance is no respecter of persons
his hand grasps a staff
to one end of which is bound with beaded red cloth
a sword
and to the other
more feathers

the drum looks like a large wooden grain-measure
the ends covered with parchment
painted half black, half red
booms from the red walls of the dancing lodge
the sneaking dogs snarl and scuffle over the scraps
tossed from the tents
perhaps a shot goes off by accident
sending a hard chilling note
through the camp's drowsing voices
Four-Sky Thunder,ᶠpainkiller drugged
trolls tipsily in a near-by lodge
the red-handed assassins got a sort of moral bracing
the red glow

f) Four-Sky Thunder (Cree, Frog Lake—Big Bear's band) was sent to prison for a term
varying from two to fourteen years.

The red-blood sun or,
The sun had scorched its green roofing leaves was sinking

In his veins
we should surely be killed
but if not too close to a white man
he might be spared
something in all this that gets into the blood
of his white-skinned brother and sticks there
surged to his face and made it dark
was still upon the blade
got beyond my control and shed the blood
melted the man of blood
spill blood, plenty Canadian
rapid rise and spread of the revolt
and the shedding of blood
he was big and burly and showed his
mixed precious blood to drown
a pure blood Cree
mounting a knoll
read in rounded English periods
from a manuscript

a redcoat scout was reported on the rim of the coulee
and pandemonium
his face gaudy with red and yellow
a trait of the red man
and streamers of red and white calico
that weakness for a tawny oval face
was a failing of too many of the white men
whom the government employed
to show the ignorant red man
how to live red or white
he went on to speak of the troubles of the spring
and pointing to a short red-haired policeman before him
this little fox is always barking at my heels
a magnificent type of the American red man
white or red whenever he opened his mouth
a weird, melancholy strain came to me
kindly red folk of the Plains
the red man will give back only the peaceful whistle of the locomotive

The ordinary red man

The Queen[g] paced the floor filled the office packed the hall
the stairs the doors and the open windows
trailed away into the square between the buildings
carried guns under her blanket, disfigured with red

and yellow paint, the Queen felt much annoyed
The guns belonged to the Queen, and the sun
flashed on her polished carbines, the sun studded
with brass nails, a dull red pool glowing murkily in the socket

Her red child nostrils thick galloping
the painted chin his lips thin and straight
and face as long as a flour barrel, from his guns
ochre bullets sang, profusely beaded

He walks along the red blossoms of Scarlet beans
Minnesota sweet corn and his gun-mouth reports
the red sun sank lying softly
in the deep-set twinkling black eye

g) Queen Victoria (Reign 1837–1901, United Kingdom) has councillors who
are men.

With the knife-blades of a pukamakin
the grass tears up, beneath it stretch two iron lines
its scalp pieces, thrown out on both sides
of the iron road, he tucks under his belt

In a wagon he places his hands, fingers
the officer's helmet, flicks a package of tea
pokes his carbine in a face whose sunlit slopes
glow from a scarlet coat and a blood-red sun

There will be a bullet there, a finger to his throat
his legs streaked with white mud, a form on the road
the dried skin of a felt hat, shook unsoldierly
folded umbrellas flashed open before the muzzle of the horse

The Indian's day swung its heavy Colt's pistol
made the eyelash flicker, the plaits of black hair
flicker, the Indian's crisp new notes lie down
while grass grew and water ran

Among the valuable things

A cask of sugar
a chest of tea
a princely fur
a bolt of calico
a caddy of tobacco
a keg of nails
it was all one

Tins of Crosse & Blackwell's
Yarmouth Bloaters
jars of pickled walnuts
and pâté de foie gras
imported at great expense
all the way from London
were slashed open with knives

sniffed at and flung on the ground

Entering the lodge of a Wood Cree

The woman occupying it
all weeping
made me tea
and gave me a cup

I took the hand that
had sped the bullets
lifted gun-hammers
had loosed the ball

They had watches
belonging to the murdered men
one, Papamakeesik
held out a watch

and asked me the time
It was eleven o'clock

Oh, Sun,

If you are kind to our children to-day
I will show you a looking-glass
what Sun wanted with a looking-glass
was too many for me then and is yet
unless the wrinkled dame believed that
like a woman, he would do anything
for a glance at his own face
he died before another sun
rose upon his bed of torture

All that remained of the H.B. Co's business at Frog Lake

I left that key hanging
in a poplar bluff

in the pocket of a discarded
pair of trousers

Perhaps some archaeologist
will discover it and write
an interesting thesis
showing how it came there

and when
and deducing from the fact
that they made locks
and must therefore have lived in houses

proofs of the high state of civilization
of the mound-builders

Bullets

sang in my ears or buried themselves in my flesh, bullets
fell back into the embrace of that wilderness, bullets
slept beneath the grasstopped hillsides and ash, bullets
covered the ground whereupon stood their habitations

The savage author of its desolation shunned a spot where in the dark
his unquiet fancy conjured up these accusing shades

The curtain drop on the last scene
in this grim, emotional drama

A sharp sound of grating iron
the trap dropped and eight bodies shot through it
a sickening click
of dislocated necks
and they hung dangling and gyrating
slowly at the ends of as many hempen lines
a few convulsive shudders

Tape B

cowan, i remember cowan,[1] he was serving
there at frog lake that time, at frog lake[2]
yes, about six,[3] yes,[4] to fort pitt, yes well

now, i guess about, about that time, them
indian tribes started to, to raise, you know
quite a something, so, some one told some

there that, told the other ones, you know, that
only, if the policemen would leave there
then it might be all right, might be better off

would not be no breakdown, that's, that's why
they went there for, fort pitt,[5] and then
from there again they left, went to battleford[6]

from fort pitt, you know, you, uh, they scout
way down and they were, so this here cowan
he was out coming all, you know, scouting

[1]   Cowan, yes.[h]
[2]   Yes, right, and there were five
      mounted policemen there all together? Five or six?
[3]   About six? But shortly before April 2nd
      they left Frog Lake?
[4]   And they went down to Fort Pitt?
[5]   I see.
[6]   From Fort Pitt.

h) David Latimer Cowan (Constable NWMP, Fort Pitt) was killed.

you know, and there was two braves and
cowan, these indians too, went down, took
another trail, that's how he came to get killed[7]

yes, the indians was at fort pitt, you know
and cowan he was out, came another guy, so
they were, fort pitt is a low, down place

you know, right there at the river and when
they come to there, you know, the indians
were all blocked the road, to get to fort pitt

it was blocked,[8] the indians?[9] oh there were
many, quite a few there, must have been
maybe a hundred or more, but they are not all

there, you know, so that's the way cowan
got killed, he run through the indian's camp
you know, i was not there,[10] at frog lake, yes

[7]   He bumped into the Indians?
[8]   How many Indians, Mr Pritchard?
[9]   How many Indians?
[10] You weren't there?
      You were still back at Frog Lake?

we came down there,[1] no, no, he came down
to battleford, we worked down this way
you know, we was all over,[2] no, no, no, no

everything was quiet then, you know,[3] no
it was all over, you know,[4] that was only after
it was all over in this spot, only big bear's

they was all alone like, just, it was all over
peace, they had made, you know, and it was
only then that was fighting, like, that's the way

the policemen, that's how they went to fight
them, yes, yes,[5] oh, yes, oh, yes, i know that
poundmaker,[6] tom quinn,[7] oh, yah, big bear[8]

30

[1] I see, did your father stay in Frog Lake?
[2] Yes, but where then?
     Shortly after, were you working?
     You weren't working
     for the missionaries
     any more, were you?
[3] No more fighting at Battleford here?
[4] Ah yes, they held a trial
     of the Indians here.
[5] You, you met Poundmaker, too,
     I suppose, sometime?
[6] You have seen these pictures?
     You've seen?
[7] Yes, Tom Quinn, and?
[8] No, no, that's Ahyimasees.[i]

i) I-em-e-cease, or The Awkward (Cree, Frog Lake—Big Bear's band) called on Mr.
McKay [(HBC trader, Prince Albert) told every one that the complete overthrow of
their movement was only a question of a short time.] and told him that Riel had made
a private arrangement with his (Awkward's) father at Prince Albert last fall to join in a
rising against the whites. They had talked the matter over while in Montana.

Leawood

night
$$\begin{array}{r} 15712 \\ 417 \\ \hline 14695 \end{array}$$

mormon

$$\frac{11}{5}\,{}^{0}_{2}\!\diagup\,{}_{\diagup}\;\diagup$$
$$\frac{}{7\,\diagup}$$

III

THAT LITTLE HAMLET BY THE CREEK

How will I attempt to describe it! There is so much to tell and yet
I know not what is best to record and what is best to leave out.

—THERESA DELANEY,
from *Two Months in the Camp of Big Bear*[i]

Solomon says

> I had been sought for
> I had been the object
> I might with justice shrink
> from anything which would recall the past

—

catch the eye of a man
the seated form of night
the skin of buckboards ajar
the broke look of the horse
my fixed prairie door catching
like an idea of seated squaws
gathered in at the eye, who slightly eye
long quiet ideas of steam locomotion
like meat that, in a room, you can take the skin off of and
boil a long time, changing the water, as if it were poisoned

—

that bed where eye, I white, eye the bed, where the white cloth, I vision
    white fish
little Indian child roams, little Indian children coast down hills on
    earthen plates
I must plate bannock cakes, subdue the great roams of the organ of vision
and so we can sleep most like a hill, with no crawling out from under
    the bed

—

he un-pockets concentrated workman's eyes
a pocket knife that has two blades
and sticks one blade in the tent pole
and opens the other half way and
hammers upon our features
until he, wise and good
closes the hammer or
pockets the blade or
breaks the eyes

—

Eyes

I have embodied in the narrative
I make no apology
for issuing this volume to the public
as their unabated interest
make it manifest that they desire it

—

One of them found a glass eye
that eye was the favourite optic
of Stanley Simpson who was taken
a prisoner there by Big Bear
he brought it with him
for one of his brother Indians
who was blind in one eye
imagining with untutored wisdom
that if it gave light to a white man
it should also to a red
and they worked at it for a time
but they could not get the focus
finally they threw it away
saying it was no good
he could not see

—

I peeked over the bank of his horrible-looking head and my scalp felt very loose

> I trust the public will receive the work
> in the spirit in which it is given
> and any literary defects which it may have

—

No easy matter, the killing of an Indian, even by an Indian
a man may wear an eagle feather in his head
with one or more little scarlet tufts
doesn't count like taking hair
while the hair tells its own story
and even a fragment counts, the scalp locks
a cut made just above the eyebrows and ears
a round piece of skin, the crown the center
danced over and sung about.

But with the long side-tails
a scalp comes from one side of the head
the hair parted in the middle from front to rear
on either side plaits into a long tail behind each ear
and from these handfuls, the skin to which they attach lift
and the knife passes underneath
someone, sometimes, comes for the remainder half
and one head furnishes two
turns out two stories.

And tied so, to a willow bent into a ring
a little bigger than the scalp
trimmed, the flesh side scraped clean
stretched by thongs in the willow-ring
through holes made with an awl
a rawhide drumhead
hung to the end of a walking-stick, five or six feet
the great object of life
and something to show for it.

The peeled willow-wand bears the stretched scalp
but the full-bearded white-man offers rich-
diggings for scalpers
even the small bits
under the arms
and if with plenty of time
a skin of head, face, breast
and belly to the crotch in one piece, cured
this is big medicine.

But there was that Nebraskan breaksman
a reckless harum scarum fellow fond of drink
shot and shammed dead while a man sawed
at the head-covering
which the stoker found later on
and brought it into the car where the breaksman
recognized it as his own
he just put it into water
for the surgeons to make grow on again.

—

not the desire of the author of this work to publish

> I am only endeavouring to rectify error
> instead of aspiring to literary excellence

—

Dark hair a snare of brows, small pieces of brass fur
trotting brown in front
Eyes, small, sort of, sharp, hooks seeking brass
shrimpy-looking strung beads
A loose hanging pocket dangling rabbit on their backs
and the object not within
Abandoned were the hooks catching fish, fur babies
rabbits with their snares
My civilization, a fur civilization, a continent of rabbits
a continent short of civilization
And the kindness of fish a continent of pieces, precincts
hanging over every hair

—

A most unmelodious

I am to write a book
I never undertook to compose
I look upon the writing of these pages
I have but caught a glimpse through its folds
I might not have the story to tell that you
kind reader, will find in this short work

—

tambourine, only not half so sweet
a hoop or the lid of a butter firkin
one side with a very thin skin
while the other has strings
fastened across from side to side
and upon this they pound with sticks

a small whistle made of bone which they blow
squaws with my clothes on
with my husband's on
veils, police uniforms
and my table linen hanging on the poles
everything they wished to give to the sun
tied print and anything bright

faces painted, and fingers and ears
filled with brass rings, and thimbles
a friendly Indian made me
a present of a pair of green glasses
poured coal and machine oil
on what was left

—

Write a cold, matter-of-fact statement of the event

                                          I have to describe
                                            I have to tell
                              I would require the pen of a Fenimore
                                 I will merely offer the public
                              I give my word that it is no fiction
                        I will now crave the indulgence of my readers

Write a cold, matter-of-fact statement of the event

I have to describe
I have to tell
I would require the pen of a Fenimore
I will merely offer the public
I give my word that it is no fiction
I will now crave the indulgence of my readers
while they peruse the following pages

—

my shoes all wet and frozen and the Indians came along
and told us what they saw in the heavens
they saw a church and a man on a large black horse
with his arm out and he looked so angry, a girdle around his waist
frescoed eyes painted like stars, in red, yellow and green

The Indians were riding beside us with our horses and buckboards,
    laughing
and jeering at us with umbrellas over their heads and buffalo
    overcoats on

—

Gathered up a few that were scattered around in
the dirt and saved them when no one was looking

I would deem it out of place to detain my readers
with a lengthy description of my birth-place

—

With the feathers they mix
porcupine quills and knitt [sic]
the whole into their hair

Then daub their head
with a species of white clay
their bodies are painted a bright yellow

Over the forehead a deep green
then streaks of yellow and black
blue and purple upon the eyelids and nose

The streaks are a deep crimson dotted
with black, blue, or green
in a word

They appear when the red
blue, green and white feathers deck the head
the body a deep orange or bright yellow

And the features tattooed in all fantastic forms
no circus clown could ever equal
their ghostly decorations

A greenery-yellow hue
that one assumes
when under the electric light

—

without giving expression to sentiments of sorrow

> I will strive to push on
> to the end of my undertaking
> without tiring my readers
> with vain expressions

—

It was in a circle
and a space in the centre being kept for dancing
and the rabbit in the pot boiling, it was all there, head, eyes, feet
and everything together
and Little Poplar[j] was arrayed in some of Miss McLean's[k] ribbons, ties
and shawls
and another with my hat tumbling over the bank
and another with Mrs. Delaney's
and the squaws with our dresses
and before the sun went down they wrapped blankets around her
as if, coming down, she would eat the whole camp up

—

a sea of green interspersed with beautiful flowers and plants
as in the echo after every bomb, charm lying in its wake
it glided along the large rivers and lakes and desired rest
carrying white flags, fishing and waving white flags
or perhaps the pages of a blood and thunder novel
I breathed in the echo of every bomb, a prairie charm delusion
except perhaps when viewed from the deck of a steamer

—

j) Little Poplar (Cree, Frog Lake—Big Bear's band) boasted last fall that the land would be
running with blood before long
k) Katherine "Kitty" McLean (Daughter of W. J. McLean [(Chief Factor HCB, Fort Pitt), went
into his camp for the purpose of persuading him, if possible, to abandon his intention of
attacking and capturing the fort], Fort Pitt)

Had I only the language at my command

I can but express my regret
that an abler writer does not hold my pen
A cloud has come over my life-dream

—

like the great desert of the east
would stretch back, an unbroken tract
with no object to break the monotony of the scene
rise up in solemn grandeur
from out the lonliness [sic] of the plain
casting their shadows of the sandy waste
so these monuments or tombs
appear upon the level scene of my uneventful past

That little hamlet by the creek

I will give a truthful version
I saw
I heard
I know

—

My story draws to a close
'Like a tale that is told'
it possesses, perhaps
no longer any interest for my readers, yet
before dropping the veil upon the past

For like the upas tree
if it is permitted to take root and grow
its proportions would soon become alarming
while its poisonous influence
would pollute the atmosphere
with misery, ruin, rapine and death

To my readers,
I will say that all I have told you
in these few passages
is the simple truth
nothing added thereto
nothing taken therefrom

You have toiled through them
despite the poverty of composition
and the want of literary style upon them
and now that the story is told
I thank you for your patience with me
and I trust that you may have enjoyed
a few moments of pleasure
at least, while engaged in reading

—

**When one has nothing to write
about it is hard to fill up pages**

I can relate the story from first to last

—

Tape C[1]

yes,[2] yes,[3] what?[4] that day i was in church[5]
yes, they come there it was easter, uh, easter
like, days, you know, and there come that
i forget his name now this leader there,[6] yes

uh, they come, at they were all camped out, no
they didn't take no reserve yet, that bunch they
were some, uh, in the reserve, they were all,
you know civilized, a few of them, but

big bear bunch, you know, they were all wild
he was going out there to get the treaty indians
reserve, in the summer, well, he stayed there
with these other people, the reserve people

you see?[7] well, they stayed there all winter
he never took no reserve, you know, he
broke out, yah,[8] uh huh,[9] yah, so, i was just
telling my story now, about going to church

[1] Were Whispering Man, not Whispering Man
    Wandering Spirit?[1]
[2] And Ahyimasees, and a few others
    I can't remember their names now
    they were all involved in the shooting?
[3] Where were you on this day?
    Were you in church that day?
[4] Were you in the church this day?
[5] You were in church.
[6] Wandering Spirit?
[7] I see, yes.
[8] And, Big Bear and Wandering Spirit
    and Ahyimasees were up at Frog Lake?
[9] And you were in the church the day
    that everything broke out?

I) Travelling Spirit, or Wandering Spirit (Cree, Frog Lake—Big Bear's band) entered and
remained half-kneeling in the centre of the little church, with his rifle in his hand. He
had a war hat on and his face was daubed with yellow paint in mockery.

something like, you know, something, and
this wandering spirit, you know, he, they, they
had a kind, a kind of a meeting, you know
with the farmer, with the, with the people

that lived there, they wanted, anyway, they
wanted to take us prisoners, all of us, and
he said, those that, that stays they can get all
ready like, so, and those that wants to go

they welcome, to church, and the rest, those
that stayed, they had to prepare while this
church was going on, anyway, i was all ready
there, and my dad he didn't anyway go

to church, he had to get ready, he had a big rug
and put blankets, all blankets, because they
were, we had to go all as prisoners,[10] yes, so i
i went anyway, i used to serve mass, i used to

---

[10]   Your dad, and you?

help the priests, i went down there and, so
my dad didn't go, quite a few of them didn't
go, you know, those that had families, mostly
and they had to get ready to join, they didn't

know how many people that was in church
could come with those that stayed, those that
stayed, they had to get there where they would
wait and then, anyway, it went off, pretty soon

you know, hah, hah, wandering spirit comes in
all painted up and those there, they had their
guns, you know, they had their guns, they had
the muzzles down, they stood there a little

while, you know, and he told the priest, he said
"that's enough" so and he looked, it wasn't
quite over yet, "that's enough" he said, "better
get ready, and join them up those that stayed"

and there was some, another bunch outside
you know, with guns, but they was come in
those three of them come in, and they all make
for us to go out and go back to the agency, like

and join the rest of them, tom quinn didn't go
he stayed,[11] he stayed at, uh, in his house,[12] and
we were all living there, you know, all together
tom quinn, but he didn't go to church and

my father didn't, however, that was the orders
he gave us, wandering spirit and he said
"that's enough," and he pointed at the priest
like that you know, "take off your investment

that's enough, and you, too," he said to me like
that,[13] yah, ha ha, ha, "and you too," he said "hang
up those things," so, i took off my investment
there now, to join those that stayed in the agency

[11] Yes, in the church?
[12] Yes, yes.
[13] To you, he said?

anyway, we didn't have to go home, you know
to go to our house like my dad then, we had to
stay, those that stayed had to go about a hundred
yards, we were all standing waiting for it

we stood, but i come along, you know, i come
up, i don't know, it was quite close to my father's
house pretty close, just a few yards and then
anyway, i switched off from these bunch here

heh, heh, run to my, to my dad's place and then
i didn't even o—, i just opened the door, just
opened the door, to go in, you know, my dad
wasn't quite ready yet to join then, but he was

nearly ready, but this hero kind of stuff , you
know, kind of a rowdy, what they made there
anyway, i run in, in the house and then
and then tom quinn was standing, let me see

he was standing at the door,[14] of the agency, yes
my father next, his place just between them, um
an Indian, uh wandering spirit was talking to him
wanted them to join, come and join, so he said

i heard him say and, i kind of stopped
you know, i heard him say, if you like your life
you better go over there or you won't see the
the sundown, you'll never see him, mind you

however, no, he just stood there, and then
i ran in the house,[15] he killed him, he killed
the indian agent,[16] yah, so another guy falls in
right behind me like, i don't know where he

came from, he must have come from the bunch
that was waiting there, he was a carpenter
charlie gouin his name was,[17] gouin, charlie
gouin, he was a carpenter at the indian agency

[14]   Of the agency?
[15]   Yes?
[16]   Quinn?
[17]   Gouin?[m]

51

m) Charles Gouin (Carpenter, Frog Lake), who was an American Half-breed, was shot
by the Worm immediately after on the road to the Indian camp, a short distance from
Pritchard's house.

11426
325 -
————
11751

325 -

22224
325 -
————
22549 . 13573
325 -
————
13898

0570
32
————
0602

0839
32
————
0872

103 2
3 2
————
1056

margle traced laste faint

23862
325 -
————
24187

08822
325 -
————
09147

aquline genuine

inevitably mangle traced has

IV

THE INADVERTENT POETRY OF MAJOR-GENERAL THOMAS BLAND STRANGE

The first outbreak of Indians was at Frog Lake. An Indian had been imprisoned for stealing beef said to have been put in his way by an agent. While undergoing imprisonment, his squaw became intimate with the prosecutor. When the Indian had served his term of imprisonment he returned and the agent was shot. So the massacre began. After the last fight the squaw was found hung in our line of march, also the dog of the agent, and all white prisoners were released. So it ended, as far as the Indians were concerned.

—THOMAS BLAND STRANGE,
from *Gunner Jingo's Jubilee*

It was the reign of King Cash-balance. Quantities of guns shot, and shell were sold to Yankee contractors, the barrack furniture to Jews and the very sentry-boxes shipped home with the departing troops.

The flag, however, was not sold. It was handed over to Jingo.

An additional reason for the employment of apparently unintelligible messages is found in the charges of submarine cables which has rendered those using them alive to the fact that by a well-selected code, one word or figure may be made to represent much more than it expresses:

The Queen is the supreme power in the Realm
The message thus being transmitted:—

Bounteous wedge
purifying bounteous biography
transparent posed
bounteous yoke

Plenty judging diatribe
plenty perspective inciter
crispate plenty lagoon

Talking remonstrated kinks
talking starch promised
imparted talking quote

Blundered waft
presage blundered basalt
tadpole pneumonia blundered why

Pillaging jackass
darn pillaging posing
hulk cousin pillaging ketch

Begged bulging freak
catamaran beneath
bedstead build corrupting
claimed beneath autumn few

Bends celestially fivefold brigade
bays Brazilian catalogue
conjecturing come bays
Areopagus few

Beneath celibate fixedness
brigandine beaconage breadth
catch conjugation comfort
beaker argument fiddler

Argentine decay antispasmodic
conclude beaconage anomalous
constitutional dissenter caffre
ascribable anneal cupping

Our Jingo found himself on the deck of a steamer

The grey citadel on the rock
loomed dark against the flush of sunset
that turned to burnished copper
the glittering tin roofs and spires
of the quaint old city of Quebec
and transformed the tranquil river
into molten metal
while the ships and craft along the quays
and the tall buildings stood
in violet and purple shadows

The leafless trees of Spenserwood sparkled
with the icicles of a 'verglas'
which coated every twig
and made the forest monarchs look
like chandeliers turned upside down

56

Our Jingo and B Battery reach the ice cone at Montmorency

One blizzardy day
with the flaps of their fur caps down

veering about before the wind
with coats held open, sailwise

the musical ring of their skates
invigorated by the champagney feeling of the air

the wind blew till it caught one's breath
and literally shut one's mouth
by freezing moustache and beard together

and each looked
for the dead white spot on his neighbour

The downward slide may come off
away out into the sunshine
over the level plain at the foot of the cone
or back into the seething cauldron of foam
where the river shoots with ceaseless
thunder and vibration over the edge of the precipice
while the mist rises in rainbow and spans the black abyss

Rough Work:
Rumour to-night Indians being tampered with[†]

appointing flippancy
overbearing armistice
tasting worded individuals
nonsense sullied neology
beckoned aqueous as bastion
mediate hearing totter
beckoned maimed annals
evacuation relaxation vents
shrunk commented nonsense

bids tomb totter decease
worded learned annals
forbade oppose forenoon
alluding Albert
totter abandon
manoeuvred withdraw
tyro overbearing
artery shrunk beckoned
serious baking

[†]   March 18, 1885

The fibre of the iron had crystallised

The electric aurora borealis was flushing outside
making the telegraph needles dance
while the bugle notes
had no spirit-stirring war clang about them

The pink flush of aurora borealis
swept softly upwards to the steel-blue zenith
putting out the stars that scintillated so sharply
in the still midnight sky
they looked like glory holes in the firmament
giving glimpses of an infinite radiance beyond

Rough Work:
Endeavouring to secure additional mountain guns[†]

am endeavouring to secure
arrangement nozzle hoists

i have outraging renal priestess overhaul
parried raphael
unflagging Carlton
shatter turkey

embarrassed lamentation brake
unauthorized
soapy purplish artisan revised
outlay gelatinous
umber prudential
have you any suggestions?

[†]   March 19, 1885

Not a blade of grass for a hundred miles

The horses do not suffer
they paw themselves pasture
which the cattle cannot do
snow freezes in the cleft hoof
and lames them

The helpless cattle drift
before the blizzards
and finding no shelter
on the treeless prairie
they smother
in the snow-filled coulees

But under the snow
which the warm chinook wind
soon melted
the country was found to be burnt

Rough Work:
The safety and peace in this country will be jeopardized[†]

permanent circles
who agreed to meet me
here today hyphen
outraging conjugal
innuendo before Denny
left impressed on their
importance of palpitate
irreconcilable
soapy astronomy
Crees pasturage
caul number

subjoining from Sly
Liquefying to ghouls
of Requiem Dictator
Scarlatina I consider
that the selecting
acid pitchy in this
section of country
will be harder
independence Cree Indians
mingling to get into brush
gazed camp and fearlessness

there I foretaste
ultimately Crees will
make betwixt gelatinous
Depression Imperials
acid that resident well
begum to lauded with them
there when troops gel
outlay my opinion
is shorn and by orchid
which has religiously

mitigation through
Father Lagal ultimately
umber Gros Ventres
dejected artisan
Kootenays pictures
gill sixfold a loan
frequent piazza via
Block Pirate nozzle
to Depression Imperials
Lagal says some have

† April 6, 1885

Jingo's house

A plan of a house
had been sent east and the pieces
for its erection were forwarded back
window sashes
and doors complete
all rather like a Chinese puzzle
to be put together

Sitting on the rafters shingling the roof
with the thermometer below
the freezing point of mercury
and four reflected suns in the sky
with halos round them

Rough Work:
If wheat and seed come by boat they will be in time[†]

simile ultimatum
in hood stubborn trim
incalculable angus
aquiline paroquet
shone concretely
carpentry brimful
tricky Malcolm bide
inevitably twilight, they say

[†]   April 7, 1885

Jingo's speech at Frog Lake on The Queen's birthday

A soldier of 40 is considered too old to lead 100 men
but an octogenarian is not too old to run or ruin an empire

I am proud
of the stuff I command
This is The Queen's birthday
without The Queen's weather

We cannot have
any fireworks to-day
Mr. Big Bear
won't give us the chance

But from information I have
we are close behind him
and when the chance does come
I know you are the stuff to take it

As this is The Queen's birthday
let us give her three cheers

Rough Work:
Some justifiable measure should be made
to prevent escape of Riel[n] and following[†]

Irvine[o] wires Prince
Albert as follows
striking learning moated
soapy blink metaphysician
unflagging pulling
fabled parallel remaining
artizan gathered
also umber cabriolet
apple pedant proffering
soapy blink overalls
would feel

67

n) Louis Riel (Métis, St. Boniface) looked askance at the "instantaneous" camera, perhaps fearing that it was an infernal machine, but as it didn't go off, he walked back into his tented prison apparently well pleased.

o) Lieutenant-Colonel Irvine (Commissioner NWMP, Fort Carlton) does not need any certificate of character from newspaper correspondents to induce those who know him best to believe that he is a brave and intrepid soldier.

benedictory this aluminite
on weightily peeled
friendless Stumble went
to attempt Blame Behaved
inertness communicator
too much for veered
no attempting yet assail

68

Fred White wires Cotton
urges importance of information
respecting events in the north
reaching him being sent to him
before it reaches the indians

I repeat
to Sir John and Gen'l

†   April 9, 1885

I fear I should have lost my small army in this very big Country

The most applauded warrior wore
a policeman's old tunic
on the back of which was chalked
a representation of himself
firing into a teepee of sleeping enemies

The horses also were depicted
in convenient proximity
for removal after this
glorious feat of arms

Rough Work:
Three french half breeds blundered south[†]

several messages
from Hayter Reed and Irvine
all well the latter wires
unconciliatory glossary
horizon canonries bulled
subjoining comes gelatinous
Qu'apelle malaria fish
one of them pomona tenant
weeded unassuming
artisan astronomy
others from same place
blink balloted
I have repeated to Gen'l

three French half breeds
strongly urge that these
and any others from same place
blink balloted

[†]   April 12, 1885

With field-glasses could be detected

An abandoned dough cake in the ashes

Streamers of red and white calico—
the spoils of Fort Pitt hung
from the branches of trees on the opposite crest
of a bare glacis slope

Long lines of rifle pits along its edge
the loose red earth dug out
broken branches of trees stuck into it
to represent a living growth

There was not a sound nor sign
of any movement
the very streamers
drooped
in the still morning air

I have seen miles of territory just south of the line

Dotted with carcasses
from which nothing but the skin
and sometimes the tongue
had been removed

The black mud was churned
up on the soft trails

The hoofs had dropped off
from a disease peculiar to the country
due to constant travelling in alkaline mud

The storm had been long brewing

The cloud in the West no bigger
than a man's hand

anyways, now then my dad and mother
and so on, they got kind of excited, they didn't
get over there yet but they were ready, but this
shooting had come too soon, this gouin

he just fall back, like that, you know
and all his shirt was bloody, was all on fire
they must have shot him with a shotgun
i always thought, them old kind of guns, hah

he fall in there, right like this, about half way[1]
mother pulled dad inside, anyway, they had
some water in a pail and stopped the fire
on the dead man, anyway, it didn't take long

now, you know, you could hear cry
over where there, the hill, kind of a knoll
you know, all that was there, gunfire, crying
and warhoops and so on, i was in the house

so i had to sneak out, you know they killed all
all that was there, no man was saved,[2] yes[3]
yes,[4] that's all, uh, we kept them, you know
mrs gowanlock and mrs delaney?

[1]   I see.

[2]   And your father?

[3]   Your father?
     And Mrs Gowanlock
     and Mrs Delaney?[p]

[4]   And that's, that's all?

p) Theresa Gowanlock (Wife of John A. Gowanlock [(Millwright, Frog Lake), in
partnership with Mr. Laurie, son of the editor of the *Saskatchewan Herald*, was engaged
in the construction of a grist-mill at Frog Lake, where they had shortly before completed
a saw-mill.], Frog Lake) was beside her husband when he fell, and as he dropped she
leaned down over him, putting her face to his, and as two shots had been fired at her
husband some supposed she had fallen from the second shot.

padding   prefigured   a

takens   Cornelius

copperas   zinc   me

unsettling   galvanic   ove

overset   investigation   vani

hopping   vegetable

padding   paroquet   predica

bleak   idly   ult

recipe   shunned

eagerly   sachel

V

THE TRIAL

Scatter it among the white people. It is
my defence. I am old and ugly,
but I have tried to do good.

—WILLIAM B. CAMERON'S BIG BEAR,
from *The War Trail of Big Bear*

He wanted to send an Indian to White Fish
Creek to invite the Bacana Indians, he was
about sending an Indian, he enticed the
Indians to come in and join him, and then he
to Montour, I want you to write, to do the
same, to send a letter to your friends at La
Biche, and then he says, for my part, I send
word to Bacana, if he did not want to come to
join me, let him buy a swift horse and clear
the country, the chief was at White Fish
Creek was to do this, he was ready to send
the Indian, he wanted to know the contents of
the letter, he said yes, yes, that was all he said

| Mis-ta-hah-mis-qua

**And I could not refuse them, I dare not
refuse them, because they would have
just as likely as not blown my brains out**

Yes, yes, at Frog Lake
yes, I know them all, yes
I saw the second prisoner charged there
and I saw the third one
and I saw the sixth
and I saw the seventh
and I saw the eighth
and I am not certain
about the other I am pretty sure
that he was there
the last one the ninth
the first prisoner you have charged
I don't know him by name
Natoos is what we always call him
Kah-sah-kowah-tah, No. 3
Kah-ke-we-pah-tow, No. 6
and No. 7 and No. 8
yes, well

He was doing nothing, he was sitting in a chair in
the house, he was not present, he being the chief,
he wanted to take Fort Pitt, and told them not to try
and kill anybody that time, he wanted to save the
families that were in the fort, he said if he could get
the police to leave the fort it would be good, that is
what he said, he had no influence in this, I don't
know whether he did of course, I did not see him
and I have not seen if he had anything at the fort, I
did not say if he wanted to try and prevent them,
but I heard those words, he had clothing, he had
blankets, but could not say whether they came
from there, but I saw some goods with him
blankets and clothing he had on his back his family

| Mis-ta-hah-mis-qua, Big Bear

According to W.J. Maclean, sworn

well, some say that the dead indians are the good ones
but in his life i considered him a good indian
this is a live indian and i consider him a good one, yes
a good, though a live one

i seen him, yes, once or twice i am sure of
he was doing nothing, no, i believe he had goods
not taken by himself however, i think he had some tea
i am sure he had some tea given to him

that is the extent of it, he grumbled, i don't know
i am sure nothing more than anybody else
a characteristic of indians is grumbling
it was a good long walk before sunrise, and such

when the sun would be at a certain point in the sky
had a parley with the chiefs, with the prisoner in the dock
that one was listening, although, i did not speak
to him nor did he speak to me

big bear, he was a sort of chief, i believe
he was perfectly mute
advised them strongly to leave
that they had better of, by letters

i am a pretty good critic as to handwriting, generally
i can identify handwriting very well
some of them i don't know what became of them
but some of them i know, that wore into atoms in my pocket
two or three little notes

i very likely kept them, all that were addressed to myself
but they were of very little importance
it is possible i may have had others
the impression is that i carried away all addressed to me

I asked him, hallo, I said, you are here, and
he said yes, when did you come back from
hunting? he was away hunting when I went
away from there, and he said, yesterday
morning he had come in, that they had sent
for him, I said, did you make a good hunt?
he said, no, and that is all that I asked just
then and then he said to me afterwards if
you wish to come in my tent and remain in
my tent, you come in and remain in my tent

| Mis-ta-hah-mis-qua, Big Bear, the prisoner

According to Henry R. Halpin, sworn

as far as ever i have heard
i have always heard
he has been a good indian
my experience of him
is that he is a good indian
yes, he has always been
as far as i have known
or heard of him

yes, i know where he was
out between frog lake
and coal lake
on the road, out hunting
and trapping
around the country
i met big bear
camped there

on the road, yes
i had a conversation
with big bear then
at the time i was passing
yes, i passed him
he was at his camp, and i
was going the other way
yes, yes

yes, to my own house
i told him i had seen
in the battleford herald
and at frog lake
that there was trouble in batoche
and that riel had stopped the mails there
i told him i thought there
was likely to be trouble

his reply was, 'i think it is very
strange,' the reply was in cree
he was surprised to hear it
not right away
i stopped and had dinner with him
i invited him
to come up to my house

at coal lake, to come out
and see me there, and he came
he came the day
after the day i left there
he did not come next day
and the day after that he came
no, i saw nobody
belonging to big bear
until after he had come to my house

where i had invited him to come
at coal lake, yes, yes, on the 21st
he came to my house
before dinner on the 21st
and went away
on the evening of the 22nd
he wanted to go home and hunt
he mentioned to me that evening

and at three o'clock
before a heavy wind
he said he thought he would
start home this evening
and go around in the bush
and he might get a chance
it was blowing so hard
to kill a moose in the bush

He complained that the young men had been
trying to take his name from him and that they
had succeeded at last, he was at one time
recognized as chief, he ought to be upwards of
sixty, I don't know that he could not, but he
always travelled on foot, he said he did not
wish to go, well, there was no Indians around
about there, only himself, if he had said to kill
us, to his own Indians, they would have killed
us sure, because I was into the camp often
trading with them, summer and winter, the
same as if I was living with them altogether,
and I found out that if he had anything to say,
the others would not hear it, if you get into a camp
of Indians and they speak to you, and
you said, do this bad, they will do it, and say,
do this good, and they would not do it perhaps

| **Mis-ta-hah-mis-qua, Big Bear, the prisoner**

And unofficially

I think I should have something to say about
the occurrences that have brought me here in chains

these people lie
they are all saying
that I tried to steal
the great mother's hat

84

she lives very far
how could I do that

how could I go there
to steal her hat

I don't want her hat
and did not know
she had one

He had horses, but everyone had taken his horses
and made use of them, he was wishing not to go, he
said to other Indians, he then said he did not want to
go, he was just walking about the camp, yes, I saw
him at Frog Lake, after he got back there, I don't
remember just exactly what he said, he was speaking
to several of his Indians, he cut up a piece
of tobacco, he said he wanted his men to cut the head
of the white people off, the same as he cut this piece
of tobacco off, he wanted the head, I suppose it is
the officer who was commanding the police at that
time, he said that he wanted them to cut off his head,
after they were to capture him, cut his head off, he
did not say how they were to kill them, he did not
say they were to cut off the heads of the white
people but they were to kill them, he told me himself

**| Mis-ta-hah-mis-qua, Big Bear,
the prisoner, the prisoner in the dock**

And the official twenty-three words of Big Bear leftover from his trial (translated from Cree)

ay, ay, against
charge
did, don't
guilty
I, I, it
judge, jury
laid
me
nor, not
recollect
the
understand
was, what, with
yes

Well, I saw him following up, he was at the
camp when I got there, at the clump of pines, he
came into camp, he was out somewhere, I don't
know where he had been, I saw him on
horseback, I don't know where he came from, he
rode in a couple of weeks, he had a man with
him who told him, He seemed to come from the
fight, he told them, he referred to, he did not
want the prisoners killed, and things of that sort,
he was trying to, I could understand that he
said this, Big Bear spoke very slowly, he
always does, he had his knife and he cut the
tobacco off, and he says, the same as I do with
my knife, he did nothing there only what he told

| **Mis-ta-hah-mis-qua, Big Bear,**
the prisoner, the prisoner in the dock

I am not really in a position to speak
whether he could, or whether he could
not, I don't know that he was, I don't
know that he was not, the prisoner in the
dock, that one was listening, although I
did not speak to him nor did he speak to
me, and the Long Lake chief was there,
and the Frog Lake chief was there, and
this chief, he was a sort of chief, I believe
he had no reserve yet, I don't know
exactly, I think it was the reverse of that, I
think the Government was grumbling, that
he did not go on his reserve, he was
perfectly mute—as well as the other chiefs

**| Mis-ta-hah-mis-qua, Big Bear,
the prisoner, the prisoner in the dock,
a sort of chief**

you know, we went to, to frenchman butte[1]
yes, but they, you know, the indians got kind
of cooled off, you know, they got kind of

scared, they started to, didn't mind their
prisoners,[2] they got kind of, you know
run away from them like, first time, you know

they used to keep 'em, but there at frenchman
butte, they, they, they just left frenchman butte
and went farther north, they never mind about

their prisoners, they had a few yet, yes,[3] mmm
hmm,[4] yes,[5] ah, ah, that's where, you know
they started, they left, they left all their prisoners

there like, you know, and run away the indians
did, uh, there, we was, ah, went back, uh
the police find us, i think that general middleton[q]

[1]   Yes, the two women went along,
       Mrs Gowanlock and Mrs Delaney?
[2]   Oh, were you there at the time?
[3]   You were there.
[4]   Because, there was some fighting
       at Frenchman Butte
       and the police were there
       and some soldiers,
       and there was shooting
       and some killed.
[5]   Some Indians were killed, and some
       policemen were killed, too?

q) Sir Frederick Dobson Middleton (General Officer Commanding the Militia of
Canada, 1884–1890) has been on his horse and along the entire line time and time
again. He has been a constant mark, and one bullet struck his cap, missing the left
temporal bone by about a quarter of an inch.

that find, found our camp,[6] and he took us, you
know, and we delivered, we had kept the women
you know, we delivered to middleton, see?

safely,[7] no, uh, we turned off a ways, a lot of
indians went that country,[8] uh hmm,[9] uh huh, yes
cooled off, they didn't care about their prisoners

you know, they didn't have many, anyway, yes
cooled off, so i was there too, when they
when they fight, you know, when the fighting

was there at frenchman butte,[10] yes, there was
a kind of hill, you know, and a big hollow there
on the west side, and we was behind there

we all had trenches, we had trenches there
because they were, many of them was fighting
from there, and i soon, i laid there, i seen them

[6] Yes, I see.
[7] Did you,
    did you go north of Frenchman Butte?
    Did you go up as far as Loon Lake?
[8] Big Bear went up that way?
[9] Went up north.
    He was getting sacred?
    Cooled off, as you say?
    He was getting cooled off, eh?
[10] You were there?

not so long ago, trenches, i made mine
you know, for the ladies to, to go in there
you know, and it was sandy like, you know

a great big one, i made it, i seen it not so long
ago,[11] yes, i was up there,[12] we had the women
see, my dad, he bought them from the indians[13]

so, i don't think cameron, i don't know where
he went from there, but anyway, we stayed
till we delivered,[14] this army that comes to fight

the indians, you know, with middleton
and when the indians run away from their
prisoners like they went there, then we come

to fort pitt delivered there, that's the way it was[15]
you say fort pitt?[16] later on, after, you know[17]
everything was quiet then, you know

[11] I see, yes, you were up there, eh?
[12] It's strange, Mr. Pritchard
      because Cameron, in his book
      you know, Cameron says that,
      that the Indians took the ladies
      further north, north of Frenchman butte.
      But he wasn't there. Cameron,
      Cameron wasn't at Frenchman butte.
      I don't think so, was he?
[13] Yes, that's right.
[14] Yes, to Middleton.
[15] And then you came down
      to Battleford?
[16] Did you come down to Battleford
      from Fort Pitt?
      Or did you stay at Fort Pitt?
[17] After? Yes, how long after?

```
                              140              29
                              521              32
                              465              56

     X
incalculable      · ogled              u

          4              francs
   370              180                a
   325-             521-               4
   695-             505-               5

Kingfisher         haranguing         pa
   salary             my 2)
   981              112               32
   325-             321-              32
   1306             437               6
                    762  odour
 Seed               dobsee
                    me
   send             040
   364              521-              an
   325-             565-
   659                               aqua
 throne         messafferme


              01347-              22444-
                                    385-

       1463  1546842022  195:60      125
       325-        325-     325-        5
       1138  15740   19235          720

                           15437-
                            325-
   505-   11297   15422  15112 20
   325-    345-    325-
   180   15172   15497            19

                                 15465- 4

   -648    20689-   00990-
    325-    325-    _____
    323    20364    10205
```

VI

EPILOGUE

The demon of anarchy and rebellion becomes tenfold more horrible when he possesses the breasts of those rude tribes who have never learned to respect the usages of civilized warfare.

—CHARLES PELHAM MULVANY,
from *The History of the North-West Rebellion of 1885*

A remarkable new jail

his cell is in the centre of a cylinder on the top floor
and his guards, they walk around it with him in view at most times

the cells, arranged in the form of a great iron cylinder
wheel about so only one cell remains at the opening at any one time

the cylinder, three stories high with ten cells on each floor
weighs forty-five tons, and hangs from above
not turned on a track from below as often assumed

the great cylinder revolves by a single crank with little force
such that a man with his left hand can move it readily

with a little water motor in the basement and the pull of a lever
the cylinder will be set and will rotate

prisoners have little chance for escape from the new jail
a cage of iron bars surround the cylinder

the entrance on each floor is guarded by two doors
the officer will need not unlock even the first door but
can swing the cylinder around until the cell appears

a simple movement and the inner door opens
and the desired prisoner may step out of his cell

the second door will let the man out but
the other prisoners are beyond any reach of an officer

the cylinder will not allow a break on a guard
who takes a man out or puts a man in
can handle any number of men in this same way

and they cannot breach it
until a choice to let them

Every one will be satisfied

The Queen has heard
that the Indians are not satisfied
they say the war ended too soon
that if it had lasted longer
they would have beaten the Queen's soldiers
and complain they were handicapped
short of ammunition and food

Now the Queen is a fair woman
but she has got mad
she does not wish to hear
about her red children complaining
so she has given orders that a big ship is to be sent
across the sea, loaded with food and ammunition
then the war will begin again

You know, uncle
what kind of a war the last one was
when the Indians were beaten
they were pardoned
and sent back to their reserves and fed
now this war won't be anything like that
this is going to be a fight to a finish

And there will be no quarter given
if the Indians win
then they will have the country back
again to themselves
and there will be no whites
and if the white soldiers win
that will be all right too

There will be no Indians any more
they will all be wiped out
and the whites
will take the country
and turn it all into farms
so which ever way it goes, uncle
every one will be satisfied

oh, yes, he looked quite a bit like this[2]
that's ahyimasees,[3] yes, oh, that's him
oh, yes looks quite a bit different too[4]

sure does, that's the big bear eh?[5]
old big bear, you know, when they had
their trial that fall in regina, after the war

you know, they had the trial, a bunch of them
at regina, so, i took cameron and my father
to swift current on a red river cart like

[1]   No, no, that's Ahyimasees.
[2]   Yes, I suppose there is a
[3]   There's a picture of Big Bear
       in here too.
[4]   Does he?
[5]   Yes.

you know, and wait for them there, you know
to, they went to regina, but i stayed there
and kept the horses, we had two horses

a saddle horse and, i stayed in swift current
they went down to regina, i think they had
the trial, they were trying, tried, you know

trial, i stayed there one month, but then
i had letter from my dad, you know, he told me
there to go back, i was to wait for them

they stayed too, too long, you know
and we waited for them here, regina
is where they had the trial,[6] and big bear

he got out, somehow, i don't know, heh heh[7]
uh huh,[8] i believe, i don't know that
but i think they were fairly well scattered,[9] yes

i think so, i think they became so that they just
went in here and there, some stayed
poundmaker's and so on,[10] i think that's right

6   Yes, yes, yes.
7   Well, he was in jail for about
two years, I think, and then he
got out, but he didn't live long
after that.
8   I don't know where his tribe
settled, where his band settled?
Where did they settle down?
Where did Big Bear's
band finally settle down?
Do you know?
9   Ah.
10   Yes, they didn't go on a
reserve? They never did get
around to taking a reserve, eh?

Rough Work:
From frenchman who defended prison to Riel[†]

trivial trace
      ghastliness

generous george
      desolating

100

provide ultimatum
      refrigeration

    [†]   Nov 7, 1885

Rough Work:
Although holding foolish and peculiar views
concerning visions as to prophecy[†]

piebald educate
reveries in aperture
overset palatial
treads refrigeration
any imbiber fumigation
aquiline phase
whichever conspire widenings
avenged ultimatum purport
aquiline grammaticize him
kingfisher apprehensive
affability blaspheme
aquiline led
sachel ghastliness

† Nov 8, 1885

The rebellion is now a thing
of the past, it is now a page

When a few generations shall come and
go our sad story of the Frog Lake
Massacre may be totally forgotten and
the actors therein consigned to
oblivion, but, these few papers, should
they by any chance survive the hand of
time will tell to the children of the
future Canada what those of your day
experienced and suffered and when
those who are yet to be learn the extent
of the troubles undergone and the
sacrifices made by those of the present
to set them examples worthy of
imitation and models fit for their
practice to build up for them a great
and solid nation they may perhaps
reflect with pride upon the history of
their country its struggles dangers
tempests and calms in those days I
trust and pray that Canada may be the
realization of that glowing picture of a
grand nation drawn by a Canadian poet

Crowfoot chief of the Blackfoot, like a dark Duke of Wellington, in the house of the 'white chief with one eye open,' as they called Jingo (from his watchfulness and his eyeglass)

The name was won by an ancestor of Crowfoot, who slew in battle the chief of the Crow tribe, a man of gigantic stature and the shoe or moccasin of the slain warrior was long retained in the family of the conqueror as a trophy. Hence the name, originally "Big Crow Shoe," was corrupted to Crowfoot

In the terra-cotta coloured mansion
'Strangmuir,' we were often surprised
by uninvited guests, the mocassined
feet would be across the threshold

before a sound was heard and the Indian
would quietly seat himself beside the piano
where the girls were practising, ask for tobacco
light his pipe, and go on smoking placidly

and listening while the governess repeated
the one ! two ! three ! with equal stolidity
though the old warrior beside her had
an ominous disc of parchment attached

to his costume, from which still hung
the now scanty tuft of a pale scalp-lock

Endnotes

The Mound-builders
i) William Bleasdell Cameron (HBC clerk, Frog Lake) went to breakfast, Yellow Bear [(Cree, Frog Lake) spoke, "Don't you see he has no blankets. What are you looking at him for?"], a Frog Lake Indian, keeping close to him all the time.

ii) Big Bear (Chief, Cree), with a band of about five hundred, had always been a troublesome and dangerous man, more fond of hunting buffaloes, whether north or south of the line, than of tilling the soil. His reserve was not definitely located, and it was not known just where he was at that time to be found. He was of the South Crees.

That little hamlet by the creek
i) Theresa Delaney (Wife of John Delaney, Frog Lake) tells her pitiful story in the following words.

The Inadvertent Poetry of Major-General Thomas Bland Strange
i) Thomas Bland Strange (Major-General, Calgary) had his first engagement. He met the rebels in the immediate vicinity of a large strip of swamp or muskeg. They retreated across this into a strong position, where they were well protected by rocks and undergrowth. After engaging them for some hours he was compelled to retreat to Fort Pitt. His loss, however, was not serious, consisting of three wounded.

Cameron, William Bleasdell. *The War Trail of Big Bear*. Toronto:
    Ryerson, 1926.

Canada. Parliament. *Sessional Papers*, 1886, XIII, No. 52.

Gowanlock, Theresa & Delaney, Theresa. *Two Months in the Camp of
    Big Bear*. 1885. *The Frog Lake "Massacre": Personal Perspectives
    on Ethnic Conflict*. Ed. Stuart Hughes. Toronto: McClelland,
    1976.

Sam Pritchard Fonds. Glenbow Archives M 4138.

Mulvany, Charles Pelham. *The History of the North-West Rebellion of
    1885*. Toronto: A. H. Hovey & Co., 1886.

Strange, Thomas Bland. *Gunner Jingo's Jubilee*. Edmonton: The
    University of Alberta Press, 1988.

William Bleasdell Cameron Fonds. Glenbow Archives M-176, M-2572,
    M-4366, M-7828, M-8123.

Acknowledgements

For teaching me the strength of letters and to mix & shuffle the words of the Book, I would like to thank, first and foremost, Christian Bök.

For his friendship & inexhaustible generosity, ongoing thanks to derek beaulieu.

& for her role in all this, whether she sees it or not, a special thanks to Kelsey Oudendag.

My gratitude to Aritha van Herk & Heather Divine for their perspectives on & support of the project.

Thanks to Peter Midgley, Linda Cameron & all those at the University of Alberta Press.

Special thanks to Myrna Kostash & the late Robert Kroetsch for their kind reception of this work.

I would also like to thank Anita Lahey (*Arc Poetry Magazine*), Anne Burke (*The Prairie Journal*) & db (*No Press*) for publishing some, &/or versions of some, of these poems.

For their expertise and assistance, I am indebted to the personnel at the Glenbow Archives, the University of Saskatchewan Library—Special Collections, & Library and Archives Canada.

Thanks to all my family and friends, especially Jeff Carpenter, for the variety of support they have and continue to provide. Finally, I wish to thank everyone past and present at the University of Calgary's English Department whose support has meant so much, especially Suzette Mayr, Harry Vandervlist, Tom Wayman, Faye Halpern, Maria Zytaruk, Barry Yzereef, Barb Howe, Brigitte Clarke, Drew McDowell, Tyler Hayden, Shaun Hanna & Indra Singh.

The epigraph by Sheila J. Minni is taken from *Archaeological Investigation of the Frog Lake Massacre Site FkOo 10: Final Report, permit 85 – 49*.

Other Titles from The University of Alberta Press

Gabriel Dumont in Paris

JORDAN ZINOVICH

200 pages

cuRRents Series

978–0–88864–321–6 | $16.95 (T) paper

Literature

The Hornbooks of Rita K

ROBERT KROETSCH

120 pages | Shortlisted for the Governor General's Award

cuRRents Series

978–0–88864–372–8 | $16.95 (T) paper

978–0–88864–635–4 | $9.99 (T) EPUB

Literature/Poetry

Bloody Jack

DENNIS COOLEY

DOUGLAS BARBOUR, *Introduction*

298 pages

cuRRents Series

978–0–88864–391–9 | $19.95 (T) paper

Literature/Poetry